Artsy Fartsy
the Farting Penguin

by Humor Heals Us

After everyone left, Artsy shook off the extra snow, lifted his bottom, and released a huge fart.

He was sad he wasn't invited to the party. But when he got lonely, he loved to create art.

Out of what, you ask?

He used his farts, of course. Artsy Fartsy loved drawing with his farts. But he couldn't draw with just any old fart. It had to be the right kind...

There were fluffy farts. With these he could draw anything he wanted. It didn't have glitter or sequins or anything magical. But they lasted a long time.

Then, there were fart fireballs. These were rare. Artsy would use the fart fireballs to build him a nice warm fire.

On rare occasions, Artsy would be able to summon a special one and create imaginary *fart friends*.

Sometimes, Artsy even had a fart flight and created images of different birds and bugs flying around him so he wouldn't feel so lonely.

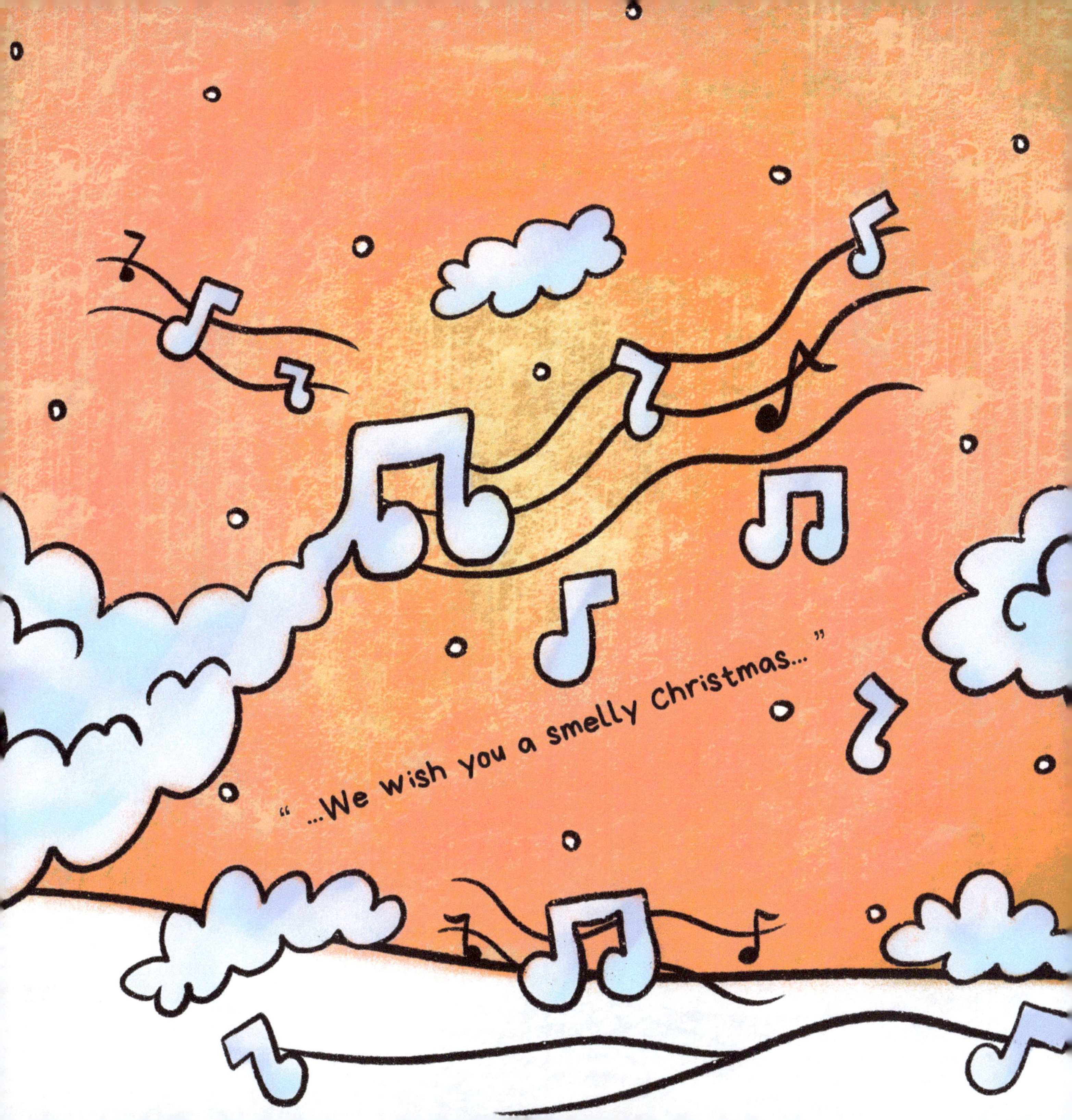

“ ...We wish you a smelly Christmas... ”

On really dark nights, he was able get really artsy fartsy and create a fart feature. He created characters and made a movie script. Then, they would act out a movie. His favorite was Pinnochio.

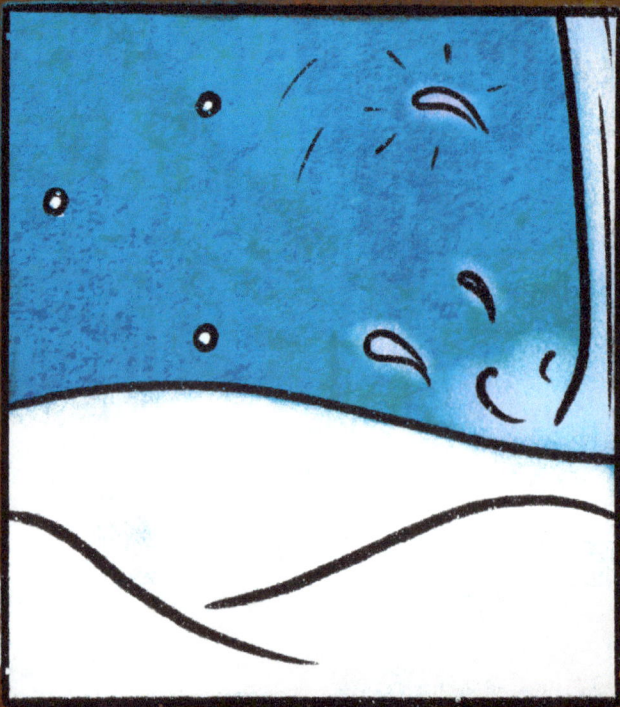

After the fart feature and he still had energy, Artsy created a firework fart display. Those could be beautiful sometimes. They lit and stunk up the sky.

When it got dark and Artsy was all alone in the yard, he used fart grenades to help protect him from anything that might be lurking about.

Even though he could entertain himself with all his creativity, he still felt happiest when he was with other penguins.
Hey Artsy! How are you today?

Follow us on FB and IG @humorhealsus
To vote on new title names and freebies, visit us
at humorhealsus.com for more information.

@humorhealsus

@humorhealsus

www.ingramcontent.com/pod-product-compliance
Lightning Source LLC
Chambersburg PA
CBHW042025090426
42811CB00016B/1742